Pyramids and Mummies A Guide to Egypt's Pharaohs

Children's Ancient History Books

BABY PROFESSOR

EDUCATION KIDS

Ancient Egypt lasted for over 3000 years from 3150 BC to 30 BC. It was one of the greatest and most powerful civilizations in the history of the world.

When people talk
about Egypt, what
usually comes to mind
are images of pyramids
and mummies.

MUMMIES

The bodies of a dead
pharaoh or queen
were mummified to
preserve their bodies.

It can take up to 70 days to properly create a mummy. Mummification is not just a physical procedure. The religious beliefs of the ancient Egyptians defined the correct way to create a mummy.

Here are the steps
for mummification:

1. The first step
is a purification
process that involves
washing the body.

2. Next, all of the
internal organs are
removed, leaving only
the heart in place.

3. So that the
body would look
normal, stuffing
was used to fill it.

4. The body was then placed in a substance called 'natron'. This helped to dry the body. Natron was almost like salt. It drew out all of the moisture from the body to slow down the process of decay. This process takes place over about 50 days.

5. After being dried, the body was removed from the natron and the stuffing was replaced with new stuffing made out of linen or sawdust.

6. To help in the preservation, special oils were placed on the body. Then several layers of linen were used to carefully wrap the body. The final linen covering was known as a 'shroud'.

7. Once done with the mummification, the mummy was placed in a 'sarcophagus'. This is a container, like a coffin, that was either made of stone or wood.

The most expensive
mummification of
all the Egyptian
people was that of
the pharaohs. Many
amulets and gems
were included in
between the layers
of linen wrapping.

Other wealthy people, who could afford it, also had high-quality mummies. The burial tombs of the wealthy people were usually in group burial grounds, unlike those of the pharaohs who each had their own place or pyramid.

PYRAMIDS OF EGYPT

The construction of
the pyramids by the
ancient Egyptians has
risen questions, like:

How did the Egyptian
build the pyramids?

For what purpose were
the pyramids built?

What can we see
inside the pyramids?

The Egyptians believed
in life after death. This
is why their pharaohs
were often buried
in giant pyramids or
in secret tombs so
that their journey to
the afterlife would
not be disturbed.
Buried with them
were many treasures
that people believed
the pharaohs would
need in the afterlife.

These pyramids, or Egyptian tombs, were built in the Valley of the Kings and the Valley of the Queens. The tomb of King Tutankhamun was the most famous among all of the tombs built there.

Among many great structures, the Great Sphinx of Giza, located near modern-day Cairo, is one of the most famous. The Great Sphinx of Giza is a statue of a monster that has a man's head but a lion's body.

The pyramids found
at Giza are the most
famous Egyptian
pyramids. Giza is near
Cairo. The largest
pyramid is the Pyramid
of Khufu at Giza.

Of all the Seven
Wonders of the
Ancient World, only
the Pyramid of Khufu
is still in existence.

Visit
BABY PROFESSOR
EDUCATION KIDS
www.BabyProfessorBooks.com
to download Free Baby Professor eBooks and view
our catalog of new and exciting Children's Books